EVERYBODY POOPS 410 POUNDS A YEAR

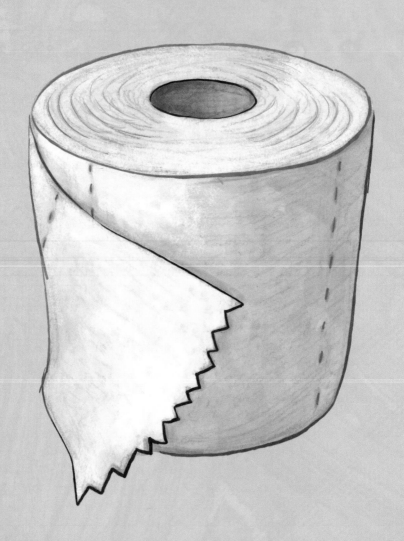

EVERYBODY POOPS 410 POUNDS A YEAR

An Illustrated Bathroom Companion for Grown-Ups

Text by Deuce Flanagan
Illustrated by David R. Dudley

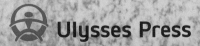
Ulysses Press

Published in the United States by
Ulysses Press
P.O. Box 3440
Berkeley, CA 94703
www.ulyssespress.com

ISBN: 978-1-56975-777-2
Library of Congress Control Number: 2010927176

Printed in the United States by Bang Printing

10 9 8 7 6 5 4 3

Acquisitions editor: Keith Riegert
Managing editor: Claire Chun
Proofreader: Lauren Harrison
Front cover design: Double R Design

Distributed by Publishers Group West

For the Tidy Bowl Man: bon voyage, buddy.
—D. F.

For Lisa, as if I haven't already given you enough crap.
—D. R. D.

It's a wonderful, smelly world.

A wise man once said, "Don't live by 'you are what you eat,' live by 'you are what you don't poop.'" Indeed, pooping, the final act of digestion, is also one of the body's most important movements. It rids our bodies of harmful toxins, clears away indigestible fibers and excess fats and proteins, and provides a vital and lengthy break to the monotony of the work day.

Despite poop's importance in our daily lives, the fascinating facts about defecation are often considered too taboo for normal conversation. Thus, too many people live their whole lives without answers to these potentially life-altering questions:

- Why is my poop blue?

- Where does it go after I flush?

- What did people wipe with before toilet paper? And ...

- Did the Japanese really use wooden sticks?

- Are furniture companies seriously making sofas out of cow pies?

- Where does all the fish poop in the ocean go?

- Why did I just crap my pants playing hide-and-go-seek?

- And, of course, what does whale poop look like?

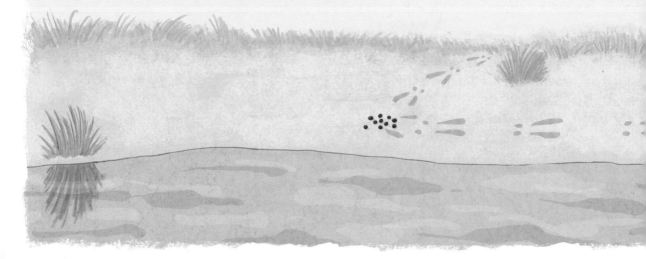

There are facts that will blow you out of the water.

Sit on your porcelain throne of ignorance no longer, my friend. All of the answers and the world's dirtiest facts are here at your fingertips. Here are a few gems to share at the dinner table:

- America flushes down an approximate 200,000 trees worth of toilet paper every year.

- Some fiber-loving people produce an average of 700 pounds of poop each year—the weight of a Harley-Davidson motorcycle.

- Not impressed? A full-grown elephant can drop 70 pounds of poop a day (or about 25,000 pounds per year).

- Bears, on the other hand, create a rectal plug that stops them from pooping during their six-month winter hibernations.

- During World War II, Nazi tank drivers in Africa believed it was good luck to run over the camel dung littering the desert—a superstition that was not lost on Allied bomb makers, who quickly devised some highly explosive camel crap.

- Before the automobile, New York City was so overrun by horses and pack animals that during the winter the streets were covered in five feet of ice-packed manure.

And possibly scare the crap right out of you ...

Of course, poop is not just roses and corn-kernels, it has a much darker side as well. For instance, did you know that ...

- excessive straining during a tough #2 can trigger an aneurysm or heart attack?

- severe constipation can turn deadly?

- the "stomach flu" is rarely actually caused by influenza virus—it's caused by the consumption of food contaminated with fecal bacteria?

- some poop is so toxic, it can be more lethal than snake venom?

- laxative abuse can cause intestinal paralysis?

- each flush of the toilet can send poo particles spraying up to six feet—right on to your new toothbrush?

... so, keep your hands and arms inside, it's going to be a wet and wild ride.

During your lifetime, you could spend right around 9,000 hours (one full year!) with your cheeks pressed firmly to the toilet seat. Isn't it time you found out what, exactly, you are doing during all that time?

Prepare to find out ...

A rose by any other name...

Think of poo as the quintessential reject. Of all the food that goes into your body, a remarkably small portion ever comes out again. So then what, you ask, is poop made of?

- 75% is unused water (why dehydration = constipation)
- 10% is dead bacteria (which gives poop its distinct fragrance)
- 10% is indigestible foods like fiber (why those corn kernels seem to be intact)
- 5% is ALIVE ... well, it's living bacteria. And the excess foods the body didn't use.

The Birth of a Two-Pound Turdling

1. The "in-hole" or "mouth." Food entering the mouth is turned into a digestible mush by churning teeth.

2. The esophagus pushes the food toward the stomach using powerful muscles.

3. The stomach stores food and liquid. As it saves the matter, it also uses dissolving juices to break everything into smaller, digestible pieces.

4. The stomach slowly releases the now unrecognizable food into the intestines, where nutrients are absorbed by the porous lining.

5. The "indigestible" material passes through the intestines to the colon, where it is compacted and stored for evacuation.

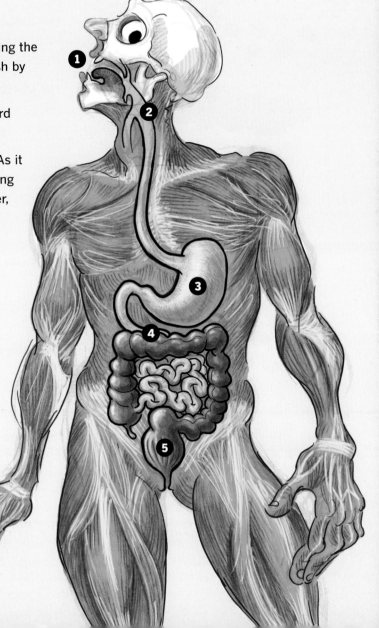

The Bristol Stool Chart

The Rabbit Pellet. For all that aneurysm-inducing effort, the bowl is still empty. Major constipation.

The Childbirth. Passing a rock-solid poo that feels more like a 10-pound baby emerging from your colon. Another sign of constipation.

The Sausage Log. This is the ideal bathroom creation, the type of #2 you would write home about.

The Snake. Another favorable deuce. This softer version of the Sausage Log indicates a tract functioning A-OK.

The Shotgun. More "spray" than a single dropping. You might be wondering what you had for lunch.

The Storm Cloud. Shot out of your rectum like a torrential rain, this is the type of poo that comes with a sense of urgency.

The Faux Cholera. If you've snacked on the ice in Juarez, you'll understand this panic-filled diarrhea.

All the Colors of the Rainbow

A brown poo indicates all systems are normal. The traditional brown comes from a small amount of bile (broken down red blood cells).

A green St. Patty's poo can actually be healthier than brown as it's produced by a hearty diet of chlorophyll-rich leafy green vegetables.

If you see red in the toilet, you either love your beets or could be slowly bleeding to death from an open wound in the lower digestive tract or rectum.

That's not valuable coal you're producing. A black poo means you need to get your ass to a doctor. This could indicate an ulcer or bleeding upper digestive tract.

The extremely rare blue poop is normally from an excessive amount of Smurf-hued food coloring. In infants, however, it can also indicate a rare illness.

Often the sign of giardia, yellow poop is generally caused by intestinal parasites.

If you're deucing off-white, you've either just enjoyed a delicious barium milk shake or your liver is on the fritz.

Holy crap, it reminds me of Paris.

It's almost science fiction: The alien civilization leaves its dark, sphincterlike nebula and arrives in one giant spaceship on a life-giving planet. And so it is everyday—a metropolis-sized colony of bacteria starts a new life on earth when your colon unleashes a rectal rocket into the cosmic bowl.

Everyone poops 410 pounds per year, minimum.

People come in all shapes, sizes, and stomach capacities. But one thing is sure: This year, you'll crap significantly more than you weigh. With each deuce weighing 1 to 2 pounds, the average person pumps out just over 400 pounds in a year. Of course, diet makes a difference—if you eat your fiber, your poo could tip the scales at a clean 700 pounds.

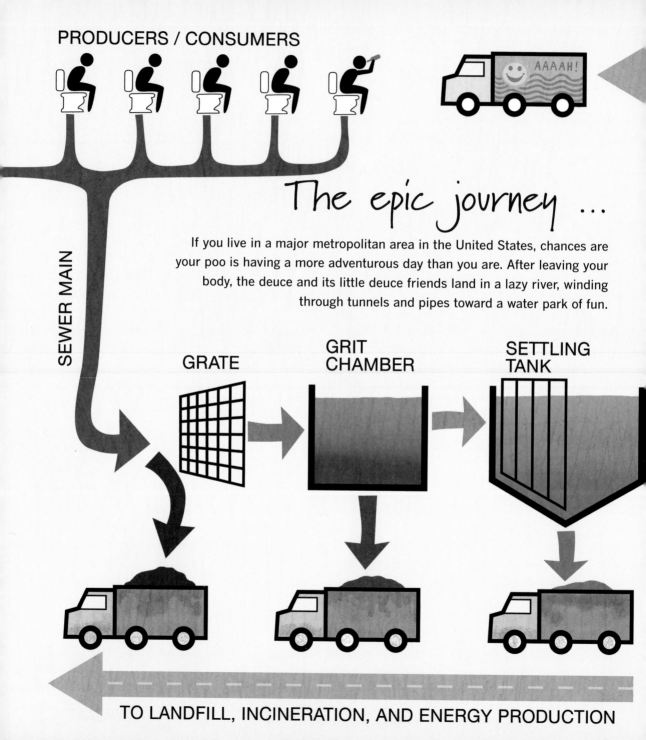

PRODUCERS / CONSUMERS

AAAAH!

The epic journey ...

If you live in a major metropolitan area in the United States, chances are your poo is having a more adventurous day than you are. After leaving your body, the deuce and its little deuce friends land in a lazy river, winding through tunnels and pipes toward a water park of fun.

SEWER MAIN

GRATE

GRIT CHAMBER

SETTLING TANK

TO LANDFILL, INCINERATION, AND ENERGY PRODUCTION

... of this morning's turd.

Don't be too concerned for the little guy; you will meet again! As the treated water reenters nature, it eventually makes its way into the streams, rivers, and reservoirs that feed our cities. So crack open a cold one to the great circle of life!

AERATION & BACTERIA

CHEMICAL TREATMENT

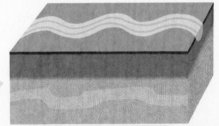

GROUND WATER, STREAMS, RIVERS

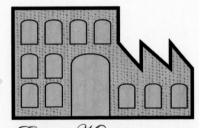

Eau de Merde
WATER BOTTLING PLANT

The Country Deuce

Miles from the nearest sewage plant, most country residents depend on the trusty septic tank to handle their daily waste.

In essence a huge underground slop bucket, the septic tank takes in the waste and allows it to separate

naturally. The gaseous smelly material floats to the top, and the heavy smelly sinkers make their home on the bottom to decompose.

Amid the poop sits the somewhat smelly toilet water, which drains out with each additional toilet flush into the adjacent yard ... right around the spot you chose to set up the barbecue.

Warm yourself with my flaming log.

Feces produce highly combustible methane gas, making poo, essentially, flammable. The dried, plant-rich poop of pack animals has been used for centuries as an easy alternative to hard-to-find wood and expensive oils.

American pioneers collected crusty buffalo chips to fuel the dark prairie nights of their trek westward.

Speaking of flaming logs ...
spicy meatball in, spicy meatball out.

Remember this culinary rule the next time you accidentally devour a habanero: What burns going in will burn coming out.

Chili peppers derive their tongue-scorching power from indigestible oils that create a chemical burn ... at both ends.

Casu marzu—formaggio di feci bellisimi.

The Italian island of Sardinia is home to the world's most heinous cheese—casu marzu. The dish is born when cheese flies lay their eggs in a wheel of classic Italian pecorino. Thousands of writhing larvae then consume the fresh cheese and leave behind the pungent delicacy. Pizza anyone?

Ten million vacations start just like this.

Traveler's diarrhea affects 20 to 50 percent of all international voyagers. Hence this handy trekker's rule: "You might say 'When in Rome ...' but eat one more calzone from that street cart and you'll be unleashing the Rubicon tonight."

The Rocky Mountain Hangover: Beer Squirts

Last night's 12-pack making a thirteenth appearance? Besides that hangover and mild nausea, you may be experiencing nature's intestinal science experiment—the beer squirts. With a load of indigestible fiber, rising yeast, and enough alcohol to turn the hard-working, food-absorbing bacteria in your stomach into sloshed microscopic frat brothers, beer can easily transform your intestines into a third-grader's homemade volcano.

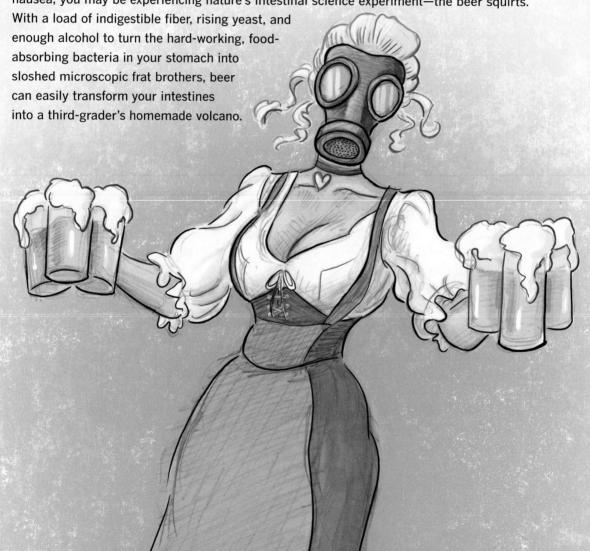

America flushes down 7.2 billion rolls of TP a year.

With each trip to the toilet requiring an average of 57 squares, and each American wiping away 24 rolls each year, it's no surprise that the toilet paper industry is worth more than $2 billion (and a couple hundred thousand trees).

What came before toilet paper?

Humans are a creative, ingenious, and adventurous species. And when it comes to wiping our asses, we tried just about everything before flushing away all that paper. Here are some of history's gems:

Before this, we used ...

... cotton, both raw and refined.

... seashells. Seriously? Ouch.

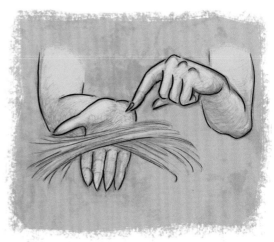

... grass: the planet's most abundant plant.

... luxuriant furs. (Primarily dead.)

... sand. Now in portable 80- and 150-grit paper versions!

... corn cobs: nature's paper (and delicious too!).

... seaweed. Because nothing's quite as refreshing as wet algae.

Two Squares of Sears Roebuck

Before TP spread its downy goodness across the States, American folk engaged in some old-timey recycling: using the torn pages of last year's Sears Roebuck catalog. Unfortunately, when the catalog finally came out with slick, glossy pages, its functional use went down the drain.

Of course, there's always the human touch.

That's right (or left)—the hand is the Swiss Army knife of appendages when it comes to taking care of business. Even today, large parts of the world rely solely on five digits—and a splash of water—to get the job done. Of course, the hand that cleans the hole differs from region to region, so it can be a bit embarrassing if you're caught using the wrong hand for, say, giving someone a left-handed high-five or double-dipping your Buffalo wings.

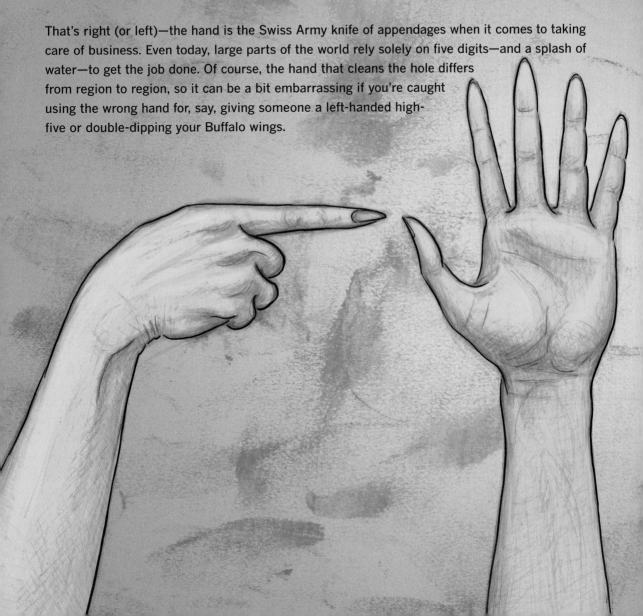

For the Glory (Hole) of Rome: The Communal Sponge

The Romans were anything but private in the area of hygiene. From public baths to endless rows of open-air toilets, when it came to getting your dirty on, you did it with plenty of company. And cleaning up was no personal affair either. Roman toilets were equipped with essentially a shared butt mop—a sponge on a stick that was returned to a bucket of salt water after each use.

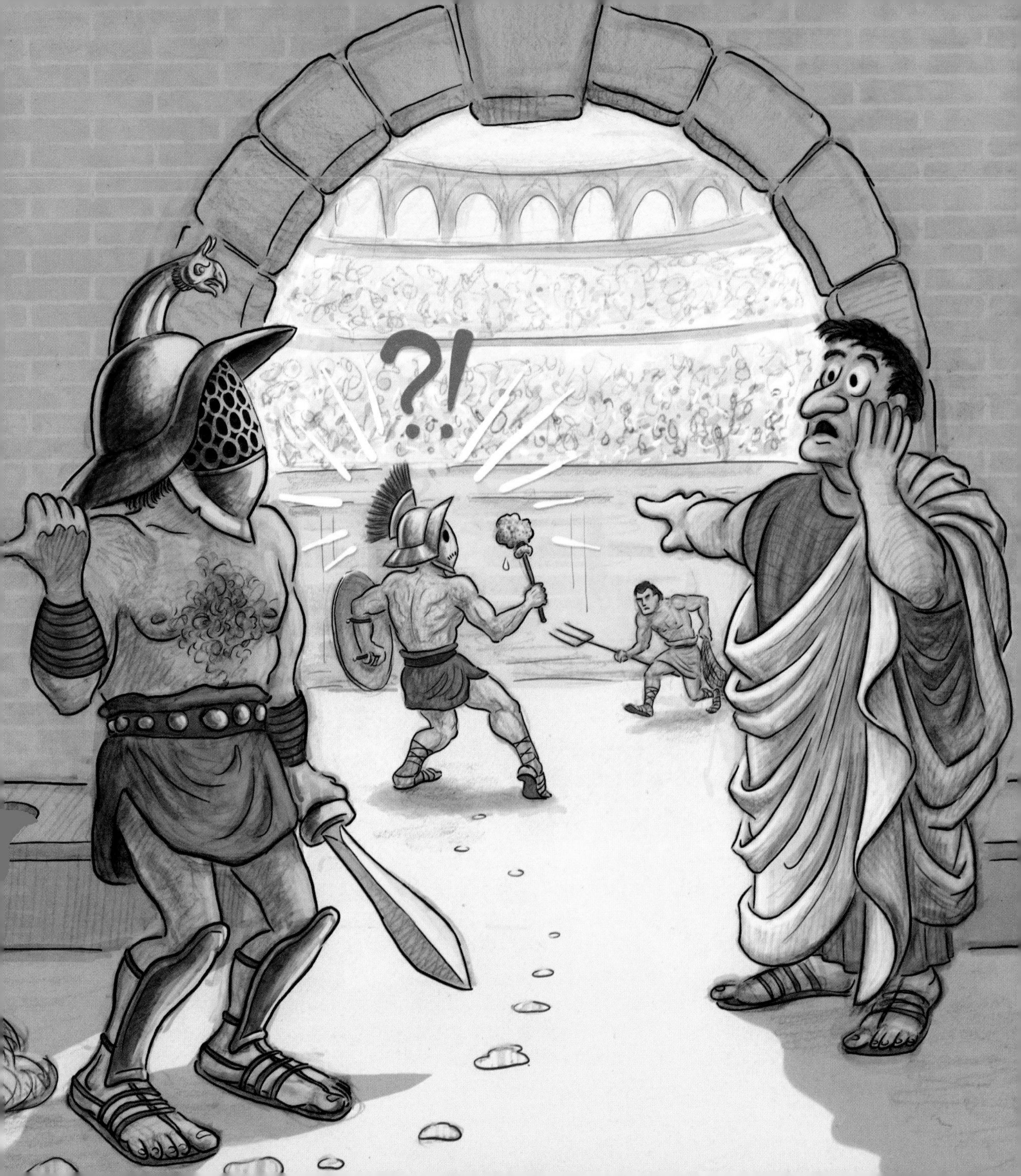
?!

The Ultimate Downy Thickness: Japanese Wiping Sticks

The Japanese take home the award for most painful wiping implement with their 8th-century "toilet sticks"—hike up your kimono and grab a handful of kindling.

You can thank Mr. Thomas Crapper for your sweet, sweet crapper.

The famed British plumber and owner of the "Venerable Thomas Crapper Co." is credited with popularizing the toilet and improving flushing in turn-of-the-century London. His eye for elegant toilet design earned him work for the Royal Family and a place in the annals of plumbing history.

T. CRAPPER & CO.

NASA Astronauts and Their Hoover

The science of pooping in space has rocketed a long way from the days when astronauts had to use crude "Apollo Bags" (plastic bags with tape to keep things in their place). Today's shuttle astronauts place cheeks to a vacuum, and their feces are gently sucked into a zero-gravity toilet that stores the space waste.

Climbing: A surprise around every ledge!

While rock climbing is a rush, it's going to the bathroom a couple thousand feet up that really gets the adrenaline flowing. To avoid dozens of flying bags of poop, climbers carry their own droppings in special containers. If they run out of room, they resort to the age-old method of smearing their own poo on the rock face, letting the sun and wind dry everything out.

This iconic image is brought to you by the #2.

Protection from falling fecal material

Before indoor sewage systems became the norm, city residents tossed their toilet creations out the window and into the streets. This resulted in some specific rules when it came to walking down the street properly:

"A man shall stroll closer to the street" has more to do with blocking high-velocity splatter than protecting the woman from oncoming traffic.

Winter in New York ain't what it used to be.

Before New York City embraced the automobile, the city's streets were crowded with more than 100,000 horses at any given time, producing almost 2.5 million pounds of manure each day.

During the long, icy winters, the city commonly built up a mixture of snow and dung that raised the street level up to five feet, one of the reasons the city's iconic brownstones feature lifted, second-story stoops.

Chicagoans used to drink that stuff like water.

In the 1800s, Chicago's primitive sewer system dumped untreated waste into the Chicago River. The river then flowed directly into Lake Michigan, which also doubled as the city's main source of drinking water.

The solution? Instead of renovating the poor sewer design, they took the easy way out: changing the whole direction the Chicago River flowed and sending it straight into the Mississippi toward St. Louis.

Presidents can rule from the throne.

Lyndon B. Johnson, the 36th president of the United States, gained notoriety for holding official meetings while perched on the porcelain throne.

The Audacity of Poop

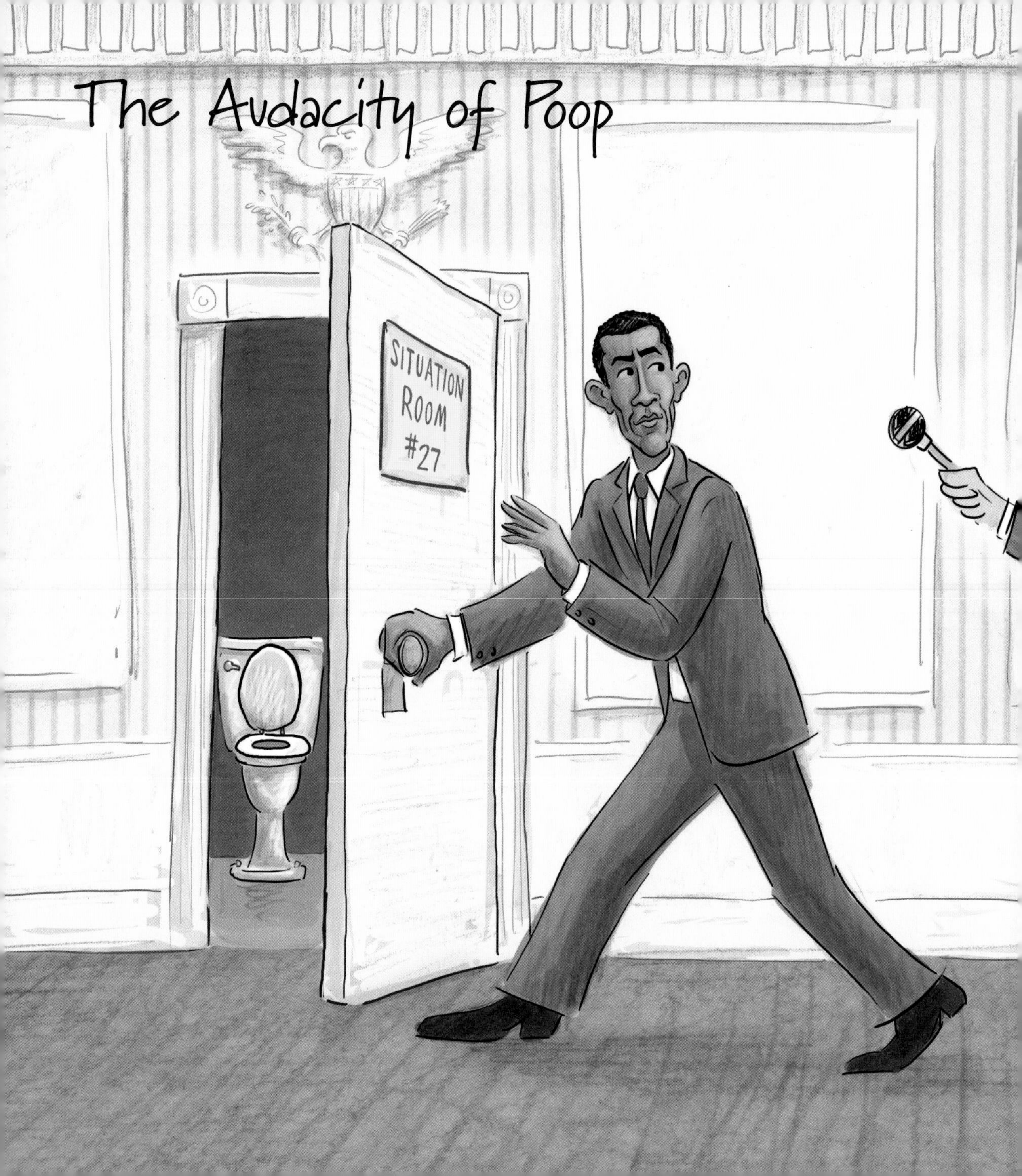
SITUATION ROOM #27

The White House has taken big steps from its early days in the 1790s, when 1600 Pennsylvania Avenue still lacked indoor plumbing. Today, the president's residence boasts 35 separate bathrooms in which to drop an executive decision.

Rectal rumor—John Wayne could crap a cow.

John Wayne's distinctive, lumbering walk may have had more to do with his diet than with his larger-than-life frame. One of the planet's most prolific consumers of red meat, John Wayne was reported to have died with 40 pounds of unprocessed feces in his colon.

Rectal rumor—the King died on the throne.

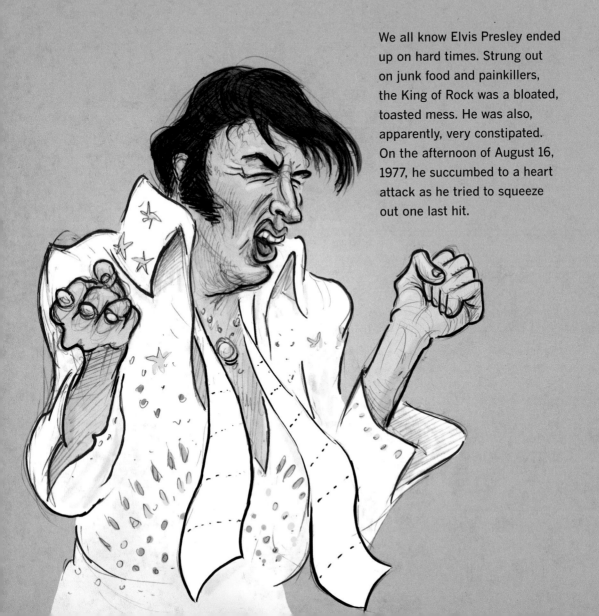

We all know Elvis Presley ended up on hard times. Strung out on junk food and painkillers, the King of Rock was a bloated, toasted mess. He was also, apparently, very constipated. On the afternoon of August 16, 1977, he succumbed to a heart attack as he tried to squeeze out one last hit.

Rectal rumor—MJ died with NOTHING.

Unlike the King of Rock, the King of Pop was purportedly withering away in the last days of his life; the coroner's report showed only medication and no food in his digestive system. Unfortunately, sleeping meds and painkillers don't pack a lot of life-sustaining nutrients.

The Laxative Diet: EXTREME Weight Loss!

Back in the 1930s, people dabbled in some crazy diets—like swallowing calorie/nutrient–devouring tapeworms to help burn the flab. Unfortunately, some of today's draconian weight-loss methods are hardly better. Chronic laxative abuse can lead to irritable bowel syndrome, intestinal paralysis, and eventually renal failure.

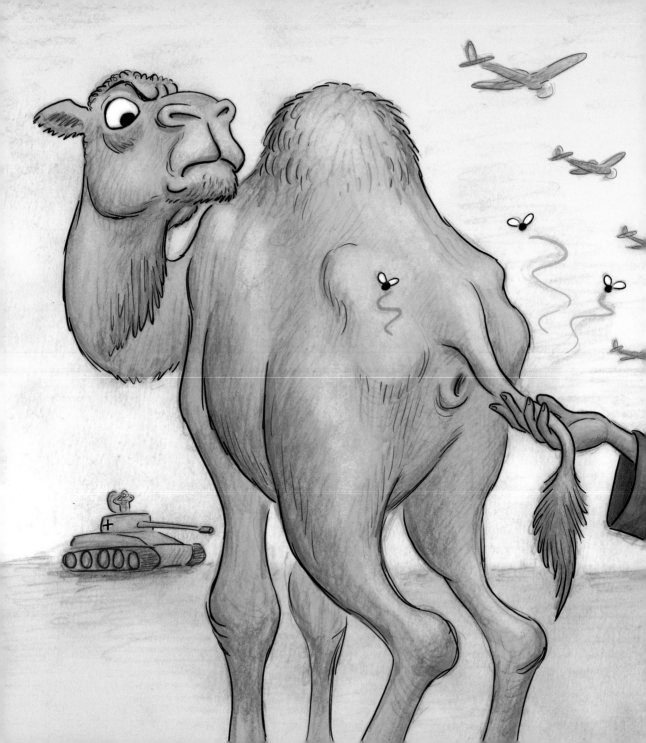

A Crappy Cure for Dysentery

During WWII, German soldiers took the advice of nomadic Bedouins in Northern Africa to help combat the dysentery plaguing the ranks. According to the locals, eating warm, fresh (and antibiotic-rich) camel dung could stave off the painful intestinal disorder. Just more proof the Nazis truly ate Schiße.

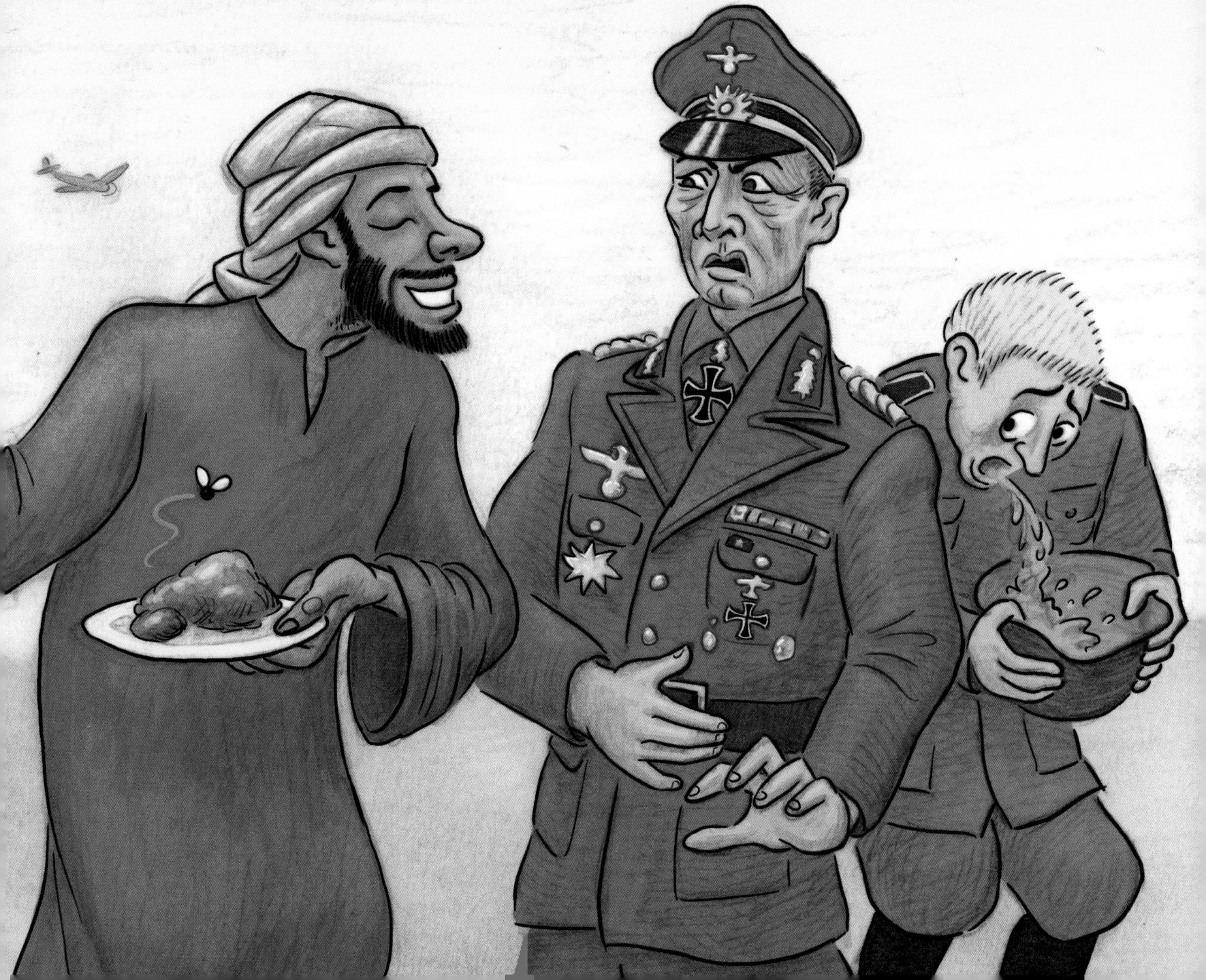

Now that's one crappy cup of coffee!

One of the world's most bizarre cups of coffee is also one of the most expensive. Kopi Luwak (civet coffee) is brewed from coffee beans that have been passed through the digestive tract of a civet (a tropical weasel-like animal from Southeast Asia). Revered for it's bitter-free, complex flavor, Kopi Luwak sells for between $30 and $100 a cup.

The bird poop on your car may be worth its weight in gold.

High-end cosmetic companies will use just about anything to achieve "beautiful" results. Bird poop, rich in exfoliating guanine, is a prized ingredient in some $200 facials.

Officially the World's Crappiest Furniture

As we burn through natural resources like they're going out of style, humans are forced to turn to new and industrious ways of constructing uncomfortable sofas. One of the most ingenious inventions is particle board ... made from cow pies. That's right, the fiber-rich and plentiful compressed turds are quickly proving themselves as the building material of tomorrow.

Coprophagia and Nature's Richest Gelato

Coprophagia—the delectable consumption of feces; literally, "the eating of poo." As strange as this practice sounds, it is fairly common in the animal kingdom. The reasons for voracious fecal-devouring vary. Some creatures live solely off excrement, while others use it as a health-food supplement, finding vital nutrients to balance out a lacking diet. As for coprophageous humans, well, that's another story.

Coprolites: Nuggets of Colonic Gold

The story embodies the American Dream: Prehistoric beast poops in the snow. Poop freezes. About 100,000 years later, man finds frozen poop, retires young.

Today, coprolites, fossilized turds from the days of yore, give scientists a detailed window into the flora and fauna that graced the earth the day that animal took a dump. Of course, it's not just scientists who clamor over frozen dung—ornately crystallized dino droppings fetch a hefty price on the jewelry market.

Science: "I was so scared, I crapped myself."

If a mugger were holding a gun to your head, you might throw down some mean karate on him. Then again, you might just crap yourself. An unfortunate side effect of the "flight-or-fight" stress response is the evacuation of all bodily fluids. As your body reverts back to its primeval impulses, it rids everything from your insides that might weigh you down while you run for your life. Unfortunately, your basic animal instincts don't take into consideration that you're currently wearing pants.

Poop can keep your ass alive.

The majority of carnivores prefer to catch live prey rather than feast on dead and diseased animals. Ever the dirty fighter, when an opossum is threatened, it plays dead and unleashes a dump with the same fragrant scent as rotting flesh.

So, the next time a bear is chasing YOU ...

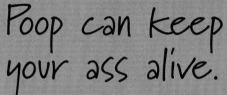

It's 3 a.m. Are your kids covered up?

Potato beetles may not be the most loving parents, but at least they try. In order to ward off predators, the beetles cover their young with a thick layer of toxic feces. Another interesting fact to tell your disobedient children.

Waste Worse Than Its Bite

Some of the world's most venomous animals also pack a relatively unknown threat on the other end. Chock-full of parasites, pathogens, and harmful bacteria, animal droppings can be just as dangerous as the animal itself.

Snakes are renowned for their fatal fecal matter, some being more dangerous to handlers than the snake itself. Of course, as long as you keep your mouth closed and wash your hands, your chances of death by snake turd are unlikely.

Comparatively, vegetarians are pooing roses.

Rich in odor-producing sulfides, the meaty poop of carnivores tends to smell horrendous. As for their herbivore prey? A high-fiber, leafy diet exits the body without making much of a stink.

HERBIVORE

CARNIVORE

The mystery of the sea: Will it sink or float?

Sure, some terrestrial animals excel at defecating underwater—polar bears can do it mid-Arctic-swim, and hippos use it to mark a wide territory in crowded rivers.

But when it comes to deep-sea pooing, humans are no match for the motion of the ocean. Without gravity's natural assistance, your internal plumbing can have a bit of trouble launching into action. In addition, the dense pressure often felt in the ear is compounded in the butt—and as survivalists will tell you, a saltwater enema is no savory treat.

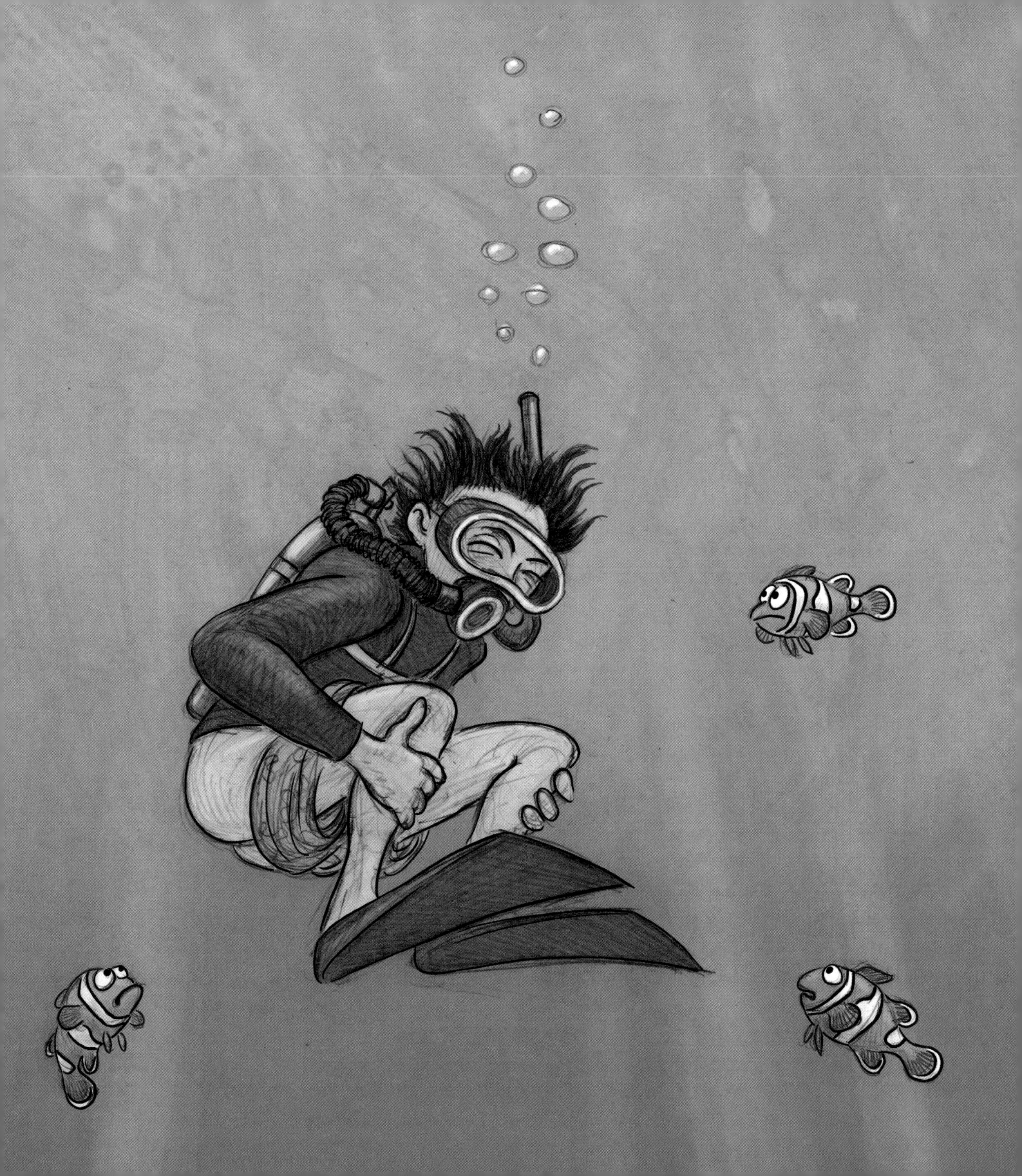

Float. It will float
like a massive cloud
of cotton candy.

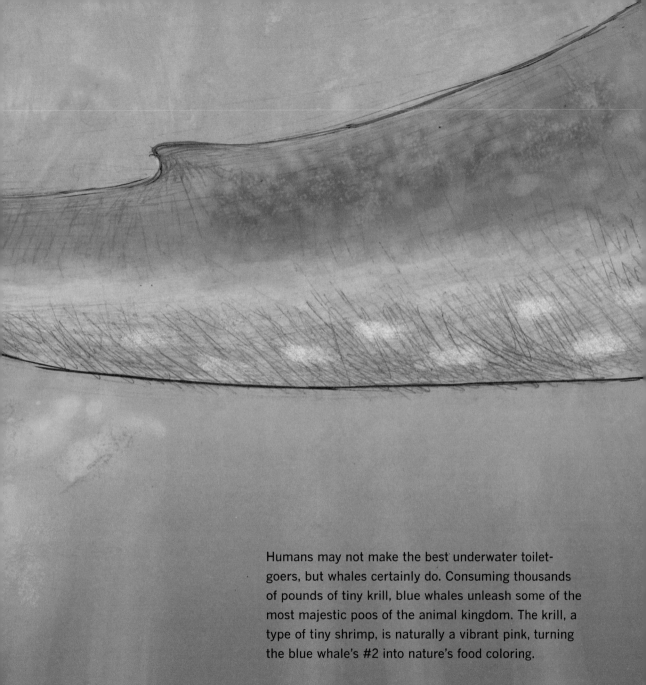

Humans may not make the best underwater toilet-goers, but whales certainly do. Consuming thousands of pounds of tiny krill, blue whales unleash some of the most majestic poos of the animal kingdom. The krill, a type of tiny shrimp, is naturally a vibrant pink, turning the blue whale's #2 into nature's food coloring.

Sand (a.k.a. a Billion Pounds of Fish Droppings)

Think about this the next time you stretch out on a balmy shoreline:

The fine white sand of the planet's silky tropical beaches is actually made up almost entirely of fish poop. Each parrotfish produces about 200 pounds of fine-grain sand a year as they munch on the ocean's coral reefs.

Conversation Gems:
Poop Terms You Should Know

Shart: During an attempted fart, you accidentally crap your pants. This is also commonly referred to as "gambled and lost" and "Hershey squirts."

Montezuma's revenge: Extreme diarrhea brought on by the ingestion of tainted food. Also referred to as "the runs," "the squirts," "Dehli belli," "mud butt," "the shits," "Southern monsoon season," and "Bangladeshi showers."

Iceberg: A log so large and impressive it could sink the Titanic. The length of this deuce emerges past the waterline, with 90 percent of the poo still submerged.

Floater: These poos are so high in gassy content they resemble a breathtaking blimp. Defying flush after flush, floaters may stubbornly remain in the bowl when everything else has gone down.

Dingleberry: The leftover remnants of a shoddy post-deuce wipe. A combination of cheap toilet paper and poop, these unfortunate hitchhikers cling to the rectal hairs like stubborn berries on a vine.

Skid mark: Evidence of a hasty or lazy cleanup, these embarrassing stains are often found by your significant other on your whitest of underwear.

Top shelf: The world's cruelest prank. A "top shelver" involves carefully pooing in the water tank of an acquaintance's toilet, leaving them to ponder for weeks where on earth that fragrance is coming from.

About the Contributors

DEUCE FLANAGAN was anal-retentive as a child, only discovering a fondness for fecal matter later in life. An avid student of bathroom humor, Flanagan became increasingly interested in the facts about poop during a trip to Sicily, on which he had persistent and painful intestinal problems. Flanagan currently lives in Oakland, California.

DAVID R. DUDLEY lives in Berkeley, California, with his wife and daughter (who pretend not to know him when he draws poop) and two dogs (who have a much higher opinion of poop). He has drawn illustrations and cartoons for clients ranging from Oxford University Press and UC Berkeley's Chemistry Department to The Bark magazine and the Darwin Awards. You can see more of his non-poop-related work at www.davidrdudley.com.